Easter

Easter is the holiday when Christians celebrate the resurrection of Jesus Christ. This special day comes on a Sunday in March or April.

It is a time that is often associated with spring and flowers, as well as bunnies, colored eggs, pretty baskets, and food! Many families and friends gather together to participate in the festivities.

Activities

Make Easter baskets out of cleaned pint-size milk cartons or plastic gallon milk jugs. Use cotton balls to decorate. Attach ears made from pink construction paper. Facial features can be cut from construction paper.

Create an Easter egg headband. Have children cut out medium-sized eggs and decorate them. Attach an egg to a headband that fits the child's head. Several eggs can be glued around the head band. To reinforce the concept of 10, up to 10 eggs can be cut out.

Sing and/or play music while doing the "Bunny Hop." Directions follow.

1. The first person stands with his or her back facing another person's front. Repeat this pattern for remaining students. All of the participants keep their feet together and hold onto the shoulders of the person in front, except the leader, who keeps his or her hands outstretched.

2. Everyone kicks right foot out to the side and brings it back. Repeat.

3. Everyone kicks left foot out to side and brings it back. Repeat.

4. Everyone hops forward with feet together.

5. Everyone hops backward with feet together.

6. Everyone hops forward three times.

Play "Bunny, May I?" just like "Mother, May I?" During the game, encourage bunny-like movement, such as hopping and jumping.

Prepare and eat a special lunch. Make egg salad sandwiches with the children. Have them mash hard-boiled eggs using a fork, then add a small amount of mayonnaise. Spread on bread that has been cut with bunny cookie cutters. Then peel and cut carrots into sticks for munching.

Bibliography

Heller, Ruth. *Chickens Aren't the Only Ones*. Putnam, 1993.

Jacobsen, Karen. *The Soviet Union*. Childrens, 1990.

Plotkin, Gregory and Rita. *Cooking the Russian Way*. Lerner, 1986.

Selsam, Millicent E. *Egg to Chick*. HarperCollins, 1970.

Rechenka's Eggs

Author: Patricia Polacco

Publisher: Philomel Books, 1988 (Canada, BeJO Sales; UK & AUS World Wide Media)

Summary: This delightful tale tells of champion painter, Babushka, who paints colorful eggs for the Easter Festival in Moskva. Babushka rescues an injured goose, that in turn lays 14 very special eggs before it returns to its flock.

Related Holiday: Easter is a Christian holiday, which falls in March or April, to celebrate the Resurrection of Jesus.

Related Poetry: "Easter: For Penny" by Myra Cohn Livingston, *Celebrations* (Holiday House, 1985); "Baby Chick" by Aileen Fisher, *Animals Animals* (Philomel Books, 1989); "The Sun on Easter Day" by Norma Farber, *The Family Read-Aloud Holiday Treasury* (Little, Brown & Company, 1991)

Related Songs: "Easter Eggs" by Maureen Gutyan, "Easter, Easter" by Colraine Pettipaw Hunley, and "I'm a Little Chicken" by Susan Peters, *Holiday Piggyback Songs* (Warren Publishing House, 1988)

Connecting Activities:

- Have a basket of decorated eggs in your story area to motivate students as you read Rechenka's Eggs. Before you read the book, explain to your students that the author, Patricia Polacco, enjoys painting Ukrainian eggs like shown those on the cover and inside the book. This is because her family came from the Ukraine and Georgian provinces in Russia.. Show your students this area on a globe or world map, and explain that the Soviet Union's republics are now separate countries. The Ukrainian folk art of decorating eggs is called Pysanky (pi San kee)

- Make a story map to show the main events of the story on egg shapes. Work with your students to list the eight main events in the story on the chalkboard. Write one event on each egg. Children may work in groups to illustrate each event. Display these on a bulletin board; add the title of the story, too.

- Point out to your students the many Russian items or words which are included in the book: *Old Moskva* (Moscow) with its onion domes, *dacha, kulich, pashka,* and *neit.* Ask students if they can derive the meanings for these words from the context. Read a factual book about this area to your class to find out more about its history. One such source is *The Soviet Union* by Karen Jacobsen, which contains photographs of the onion domes in Moscow. Watch for newspaper articles about the changes happening in these countries, such as their new governments and flags.

- Try some Russian foods with your students. The book *Cooking the Russian Way* by Gregory and Rita Plotkin contains several easy and authentic recipes.

Rechenka's Eggs (cont.)

- Encourage your students to predict if the baby gosling will lay decorated eggs or plain eggs. Children could extend this idea to create their own original endings for the story.

- You might try making eggs similar to the way Babushka did in the book. First, make small holes at both ends of the eggs. Then blow the yolk and white into a dish. Rinse the eggs with warm water and carefully pat them dry. Gently use markers to decorate the eggs. (You could ask parents to send in eggshells that have already been blown out and carefully packaged in egg cartons or ask for parent volunteers to do the work at school.)

- Color the eggs on the next page with bright markers, making sure that each egg is exactly like its match. Mount the page on tag board, cut out the eggs, and laminate them. Place the eggs in a clear, resealable plastic bag. Then put the bag of eggs in a basket of Easter grass in your story area. Have students pair up to play "Egg Concentration" in which they find matching pairs of eggs. To play, put the eggs face down on a table. Turn over two cards, one at a time, to find identical eggs. If a match is made, the player keeps the pair. If a match is not made, the player turns the eggs face down and the next player takes a turn.

- For science, have students work in pairs to do some of the following egg experiments:

    Give each pair of students a hard-boiled egg and a raw egg. Demonstrate how to try spinning the eggs on the floor, explaining that the one that is hard-boiled will spin. Have students determine which one of their eggs is hard-boiled and which is raw.

    Put a dot of red coloring on the shell of the hard-boiled egg. Leave it alone for an hour. Pull the eggshell off. The children should notice that the egg has a red dot. The red dot shows that the eggshell has tiny holes that allow air and moisture to get inside for a developing chick. Examine the eggshell with a magnifying glass to see the tiny holes.

    Use a bent paper clip to simulate a chick's beak. Peck with the paper clip on a raw egg to see how difficult it is for a baby chick to break through the egg's shell.

- Read a variety of books about eggs and animals that hatch from eggs, such as *Chickens Aren't the Only Ones* by Ruth Heller and *Egg to Chick* by Millicent E. Selsam. Set up an incubator with fertilized eggs in your classroom. Observe the hatching process firsthand. (See TCM 256 Thematic Unit—*Birds* for directions on making an incubator.)

Egg Concentration Game

See previous page for directions.

Cotton Ball Chick

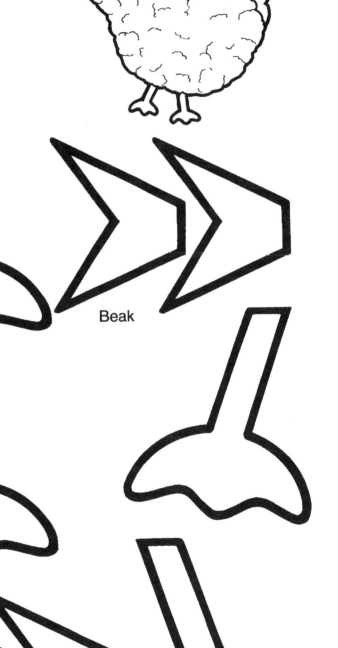

1. Reproduce body pattern on white or yellow construction paper.

2. Reproduce feet and beak patterns on orange construction paper.

3. Cut out parts and glue together as shown in diagram.

4. Glue pieces of cotton to body of chick.

Feet

Beak

Cotton Ball Chick (cont.)

Body

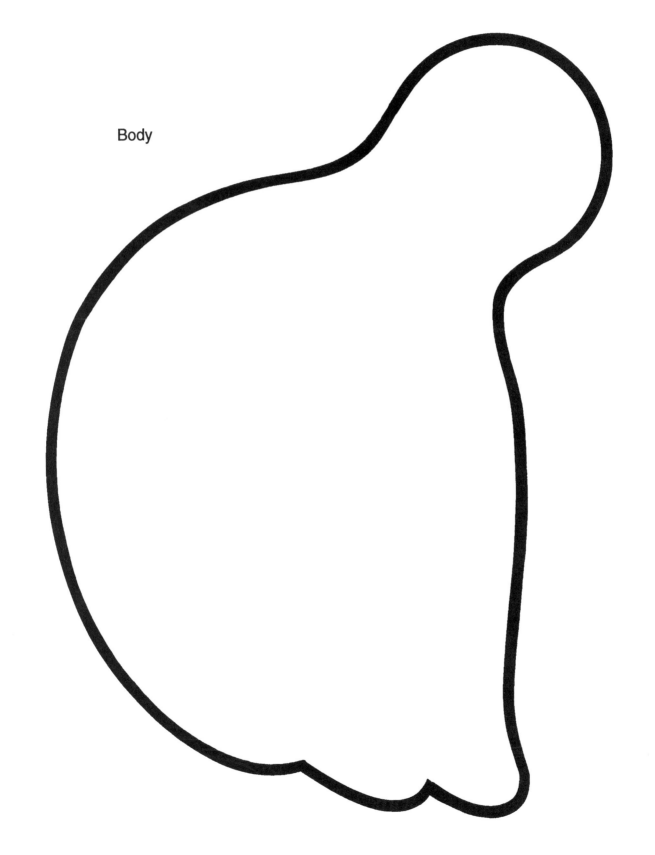

Bunny Mobile

1. Reproduce head, face, egg, carrot, and body patterns on white construction paper.
2. Reproduce arm and inner ear patterns on pink construction paper.
3. Each student needs two white and four pink patterns of each body part in order to make a two sided bunny.
4. Cut two pieces of string, approximately 2" (5 cm) long. Glue two of each head, face, and body patterns together with string inside as shown in diagram.
5. Color eggs and carrots.
6. Glue inner ears, arms, carrots, and eggs to both sides of bunny.
7. Hang string from each ear and hang from ceiling.

Body

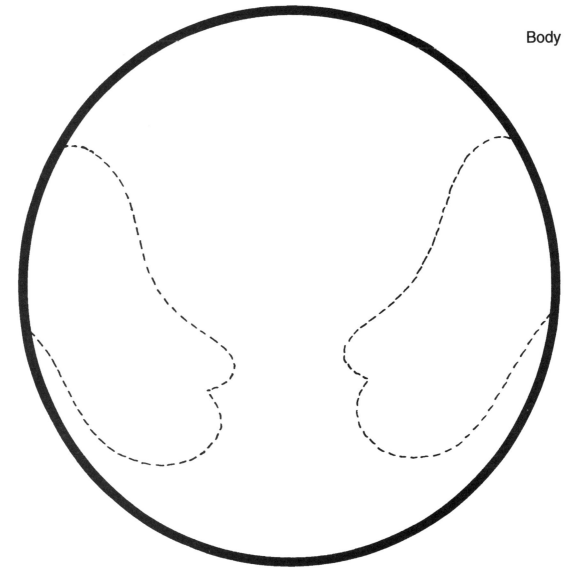

Bunny Mobile (cont.)

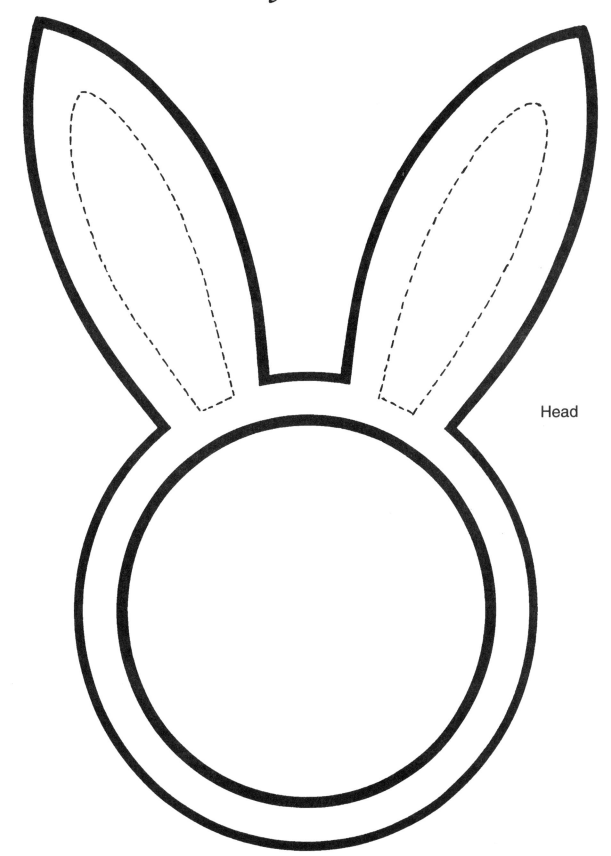

Head

Bunny Mobile (cont.)

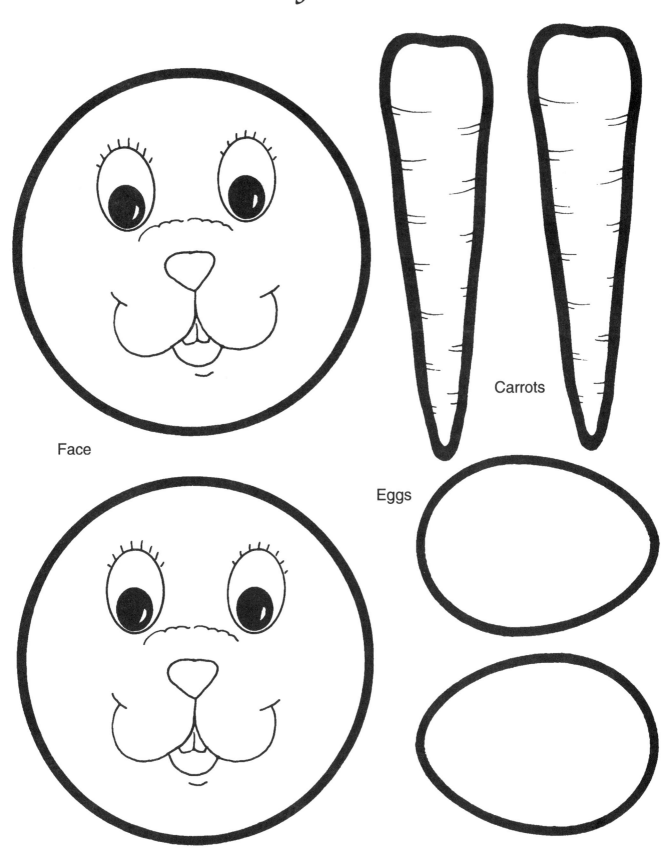

Face

Carrots

Eggs

Bunny Mobile (cont.)

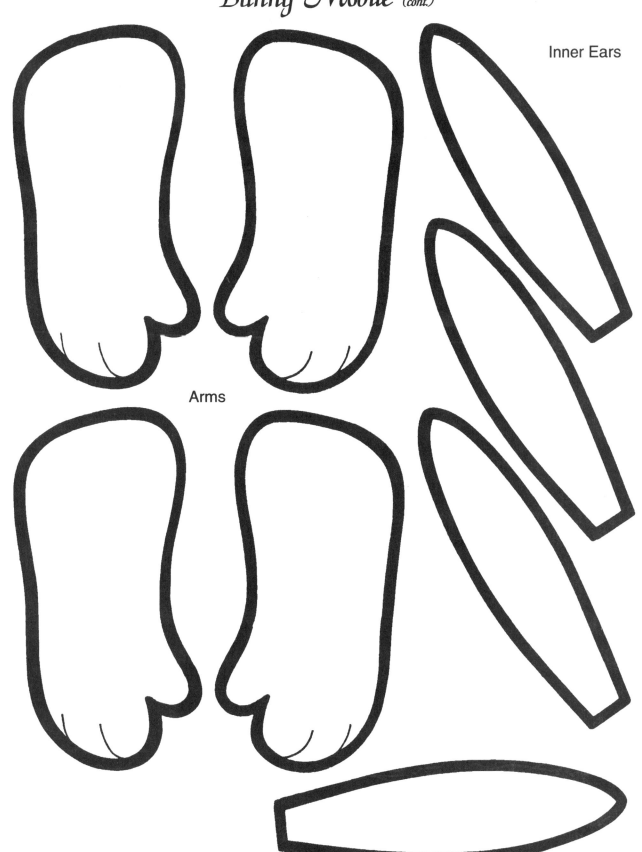

Inner Ears

Arms

Help the Easter Bunny

Can this rabbit play a trick on you? He usually hides eggs, but today he hid these items: a hat, a baseball, a shirt, an umbrella, an ice cream cone, a heart, the numeral 5, a hot dog, a pencil, and a lollipop. Can you find them?

Good work! Now color your picture.

Build a Bunny

This game is for two to six players. You may provide questions from a category you have studied, use math or vocabulary flash cards, or choose a category that you enjoy.

Preparation: Reproduce one set of bunny parts from these pages for each player. Color, laminate, and cut out. These are the game pieces. If desired, provide players with a large piece of construction paper to serve as a playing mat.

Directions: Place the bunny pieces on the table in a common pot (a shoe box works well for this). Determine which player goes first. Ask each player a question. If he or she answers correctly, he or she selects a piece of the bunny. The first player to complete a bunny is the winner.

Build a Bunny (cont.)

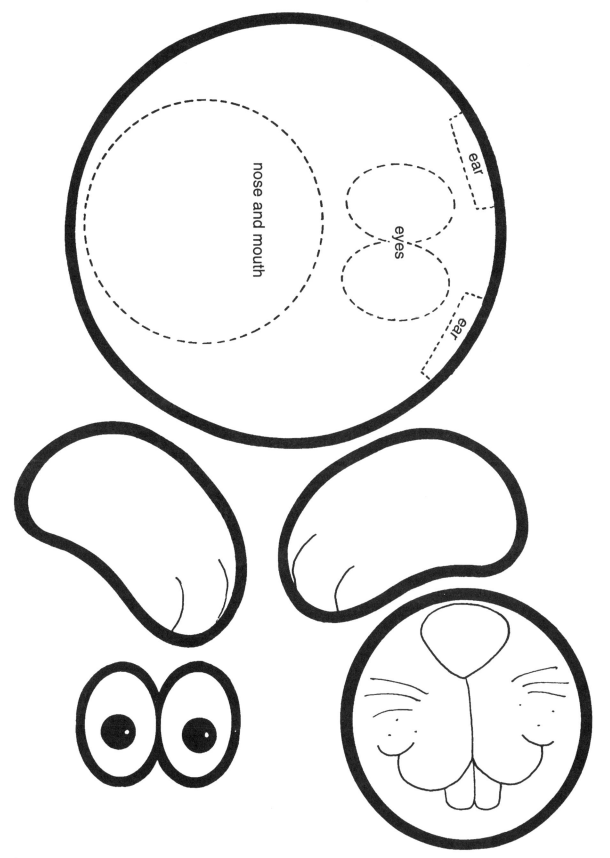

Build a Bunny (cont.)

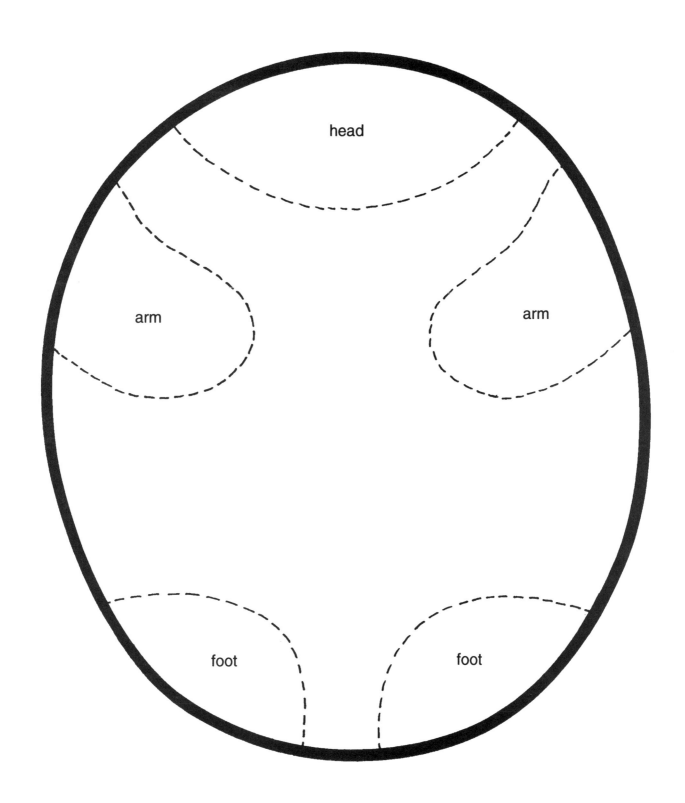

Egg-stravaganza

Confetti Eggs

These eggs are a colorful addition to an Easter basket. They are lots of fun to use in an egg toss. Simply arrange two lines of people facing each other and have participants toss the eggs back and forth. Move the lines farther away from each other after each turn.

Materials

- Eggs
- Vinegar
- Large spoon
- Confetti
- Straight pin
- Bowls
- Egg cartons
- Tape
- Food coloring

Directions

1. Poke a small hole in one end of the egg and a larger hole at the other end. Very carefully blow the contents of the egg out of the shell and into a bowl.
2. Gently place the shells in bowls of vinegar mixed with food coloring. Soak the shells until they are dyed. Use a large spoon to remove the eggs from the bowls. Place the eggs on upside-down egg cartons and allow them to dry completely.
3. Slightly enlarge the hole at the end of each egg. Fill the eggs about half full of confetti. Use tape to close the hole in each egg. For a more finished look, the holes can be covered with tissue paper that is dipped in egg white to make it stick to the shell.

Naturally Dyed Eggs

After dying these eggs clean a plastic berry basket. Weave lace through the holes in the basket. Place the dyed eggs in the basket for a pretty Easter treat.

Materials

- Hard boiled eggs
- Onion skins (tan dye)
- Saucepans and water
- Carrots (orange/peach dye)
- Large spoon
- Coffee bags (for yellow dye)
- Egg cartons
- Beets (pink/red dye)
- Frozen spinach block (green dye)
- Plastic or Styrofoam® containers, one for each color dye
- Blackberries (purple dye)

Directions

1. Separately boil the spinach, blackberries, onion skins, coffee bags, beets, and carrots until each saucepan of water is brightly colored. If only one saucepan is available, be sure to thoroughly clean it after each dye is made.
2. Carefully drain the colored water from the food items into plastic or Styrofoam® containers.
3. Gently place each hard boiled egg into a container of dye. Remove the eggs from the dyes, using the large spoon.
4. Let the eggs dry on upside-down egg cartons.

Origami Bunny

Bunnies are the most common symbol of Easter. To make origami bunnies you will need a 6" (15 cm) square of paper to fold. Follow the directions below to create a bunny while practicing origami, the Japanese art of paper folding.

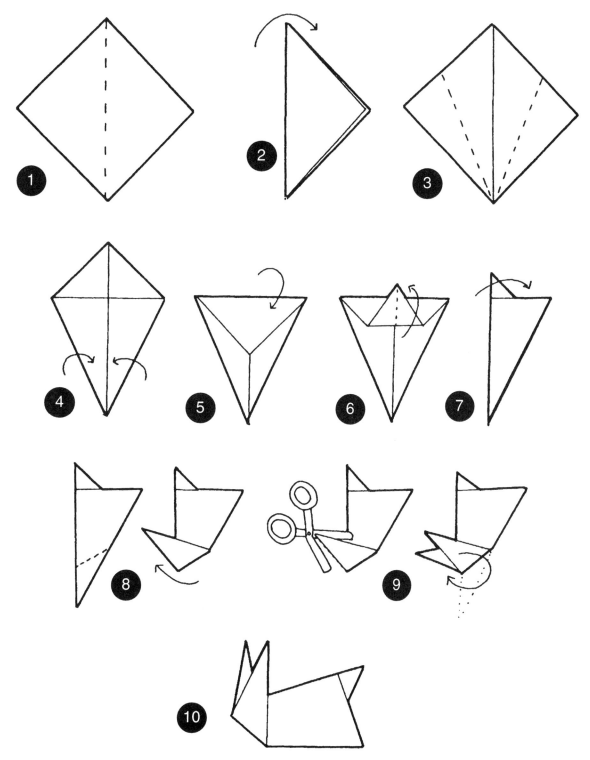